Black as the devil, hot as hell,
pure as an angel, sweet as love.

~ Charles Maurice de Talleyrand
(1754 - 1838)

Recent Publications by Angelo Letizia

Letizia, A.J. (2020) *Graphic novels as pedagogy in social studies: How to draw citizenship.* New York, NY: Palgrave-Macmillan Press.

Letizia, A.J. (2018). *Using servant leadership: How to reframe the core functions of higher education.* New Brunswick, NJ: Rutgers University Press.

Letizia, A. J. (2017). *Democracy and social justice education in the information age.* New York, NY: Palgrave-MacMillan Press.

The
Starry Devil

and
Other Unwanted Poems

by

Angelo Letizia

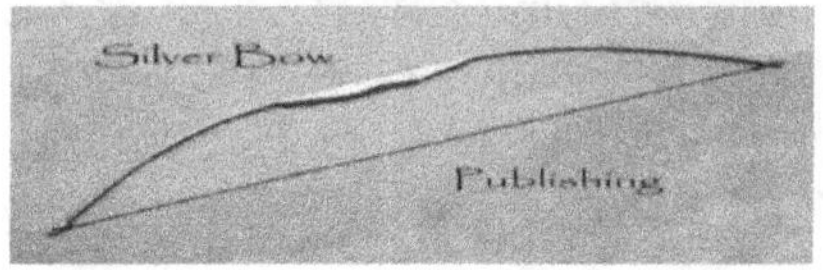

720 – Sixth Street, Box # 5
New Westminster, BC
V3C 3C5   CANADA

Title: The Starry Devil and Other Unwanted Poems
Author: Angelo Letizia
Cover Art: "Above Indigo Waters" painting by Candice James
Layout and Design: Candice James
Editor: Candice James

www.silverbowpublishing.com
info@silverbowpublishing.com
© Silver Bow Publishing 2021
isbn: 9781774031513 book
isbn: 9781774031520 e book

Library and Archives Canada Cataloguing in Publication
Title: The starry devil : and other unwanted poems / by Angelo Letizia.
Names: Letizia, Angelo, author.
Identifiers: Canadiana (print) 20210213647 | Canadiana (ebook) 20210213701 | ISBN 9781774031513
   (softcover) | ISBN 9781774031520 (Kindle)
Classification: LCC PS3612.E79 S73 2021 | DDC 811/.6—dc23

Dedication

I dedicate this book to my 22 year old self

who never thought these poems would be published.

Contents

Foreword

Human beings are bombarded with stimuli. Our brains have to filter out this stimuli for us to function. People must also deal with internal states such as emotions, feelings and memories. Poetry, at least for me, is a response to these external and internal stimuli. Poetry is a way for me to categorize these stimuli into something intelligible. Further, the poem is not a solitary endeavor. It is crafted with the aforementioned stimuli, as well as the inspirations from other poets, writers and creators. All of these components meld together to create the poem. However, the attempt does not stop there. The poem is only a beginning. It begins a conversation with others. Other people, who must also interact with stimuli, and who have emotions and experiences of their own, then must interpret the poem. In some instances, the readers will create their own poems and art, and the cycle starts again.

So, when you read these poems, what you are reading is so much more than words. You are reading *stimuli made intelligible*, specifically, the stimuli that have impacted me. You are reading the raw stuff of life, sunlight that falls on an abandoned farmhouse, the rain, a painful memory, a regret and all the other stuff of life formed into words.

~ Angelo J. Letizia, Manchester Maryland, December 2020

The Starry Devil

Bone stars
in black tar.

The moon's a skull.

It frightened me
so I worked all night
and built a fence
of chain link and wood
to block the sky.

Airplanes caught in the steel.
I hear them banging
on the wood when I sleep.

Hell is on the other side
of my fence.

I pray in winter at night .
I pray it holds.

Tar drips and bones knock
into the fence post.

Tonight I have to walk
to the horizon
to replace
a broken rusted bolt.

Sunday

There is a cicada in the house
         and my jaw hurts again.

                  Where are all the stars?

         Black holes tear themselves inside out
                  to stay hidden.
         Swallow white light.

         You have swallowed it too.

Shadows move over the mountain.
                  Curtains blow in the room.
         There is shade here but nowhere to rest.

         You must keep moving.

Electrical wires cross the pines.
         And whisper to the street.
                  And the street dreams of things
         you will never know.

Nonsense or Truth?

The lake is cracked.

      Spiral miseries
          ring through
     a rusty spring.

Frigid television waves
        crash on a shore,
     on the sand,
in some winter.

Metal caterpillars,
     vinyl inchworms
        sing in space,
          crawl beyond some skull.

       Phones and tires and summers
     do not divulge
their secrets.

Devolution

We are what was once great.
We are the dying star.
Expansion before explosion.

We are the junkyard.
                    Careless dreams
                    of arrogant beings
                who are now hairless and cold
                    bent back over
                    closer to the ground.

We are the unread book,
burnt for warmth.

            Are we really... we are?
            Or are we just is?

                    Indifferent existence ...
                    and if the gods did exist
                    they would laugh at us for this.

Fuel

There is fuel in grass.
Gasoline stink.
Where do I go?

Where do I go to see
the intestines,
the pistons,
working furiously,
silently?

There is fuel in paper
and elastic bands,
in undergarments
which stretch over
universes.

      Where do I go to see
M   A   S   K   S
      which cover cemeteries?

Fires rage in between numbers.
Decimals and jesters
laugh at our sanity.
Who knew speed limits signs
doubled as philosophers?

Help

Who will help you now?
Your head is beginning to hurt.

You want to sleep but you can't.
Rent is due to the universe.

Weary tendons manage to hold
an aging skeleton.

But for how long?

Adam's Nightmare

Wake up!
    You are dreaming again
        of mortgages and medical bills,
  of plagues and demagogues.

Go back to sleep.

    Lay next to me
      by the water,
here in our own personal paradise,
      here in Eden.

Monroe

Poems for love.
Poems for sex
      describe useless glass shards
         in a basement.

A forgotten Saturday
     years ago
        when I loved someone else.

Dust remembers it now.
      Remembers the cut on your tongue.
        But I remember
           different basements.

Better yet,
    I create my own
      in my thoughts.

        Stanzas pregnant with dust and rugs,
          that carpet another basement
        in some far-off memory.

Poetry of the Dying

Pressure behind the eyes.
Fault lines in the blood.

We rebuild after earthquakes.
But it is never enough.

> Blurred vision,
> painful jaws
>> make it hard to see;
>> hard to eat.

Arteries and electricity,
message and medium
do not match.

So I carry the message across the desert …

> and it burns
> to a patch of sand.

Epiphany in Hanover

Cemetery plots for sale.
Should I
buy one?

Bury the universe in dirt
with a stone marker?

Use my forearm
as a shovel and cover up
millions of years
of ineptitude failures and pain?

Sick.

Cracked cell phone
reminds me of heaven
I will never know.

Rousseau was Right

We reached the summit
                    only to see below
          sprawling networks of carpets and plastic.
Slow connections of neurons
                              and modems.

All your advancements in medicine
          mean you only die slower.

               All we know
                    bled through caliper
          too expensive to fix.

Leave me in the woods.

Ghosts and Kings

Microwavable feast on the table.
Cheap noodles and water.
Ghosts have overrun the kingdom
with fake skin and human names.

They all push.
They all want to sit on the throne.

Ghosts of ice and skin
and steel and bone
haunt me at the dinner table,
at the gas station,
the department store
and all these territories of the earth.

I see them in my water,
in my noodles
which they turn to gasoline,
change the floor to coal.

I am hunted by these transparent things.
These bloodless ghosts
flying around the heart
and in between the stars.

They become like kings or gods
in this ... the darkest of heavens.

Cosmology Poem (End)

There is only a glow
At the end.

Bug zapper-like sun
struggles to heat
my soup
The sun is tired and dying.

My ancient cousins labored
to build rockets, highways
and microprocessors.

But now,
I only sleep in their nightmares
and garbage.
In their ash.
It is all they left for me
at the end.

Stuck gear shift.
Unattached.
Rotting in a vacant lot.

Burnt paper.
Embers like confetti
from some forgotten athletic parade.
The only way to appreciate their greatness now.

In the beginning
there was a promise and a reason.

Now there is only rust, at the end.

More Cosmology

Blurred vision,
        but i can still see
                the black hole
                        through
                the knee's cartilage incision;
        or at the bottom
of a cavity.

                But the dentist
                is no philosopher
                or astronaut.

Drills cannot build anything
        in that black hole.

They just whirl
        and spin
                noisily.

Westminster

Peeled pavement
reveals
a terrible secret
we already know.

Bacterial grass
it should grow
and viruses leap
amongst the hot
and dying stars.

Germs congregate in a milky way
and dance all over some countertop.

All is carcinogenic now.
New cars and political signs in expensive yards.

The skin inside the pants
is toxic.
Bleach makes it worse.
Bleach reverses
and becomes a germ.

Like the rest of the universe.

Moments in September

Where do I find the gasoline?
under the hollow sky?
The clouds are all hollow now
and the ocean, a door.

Pour out the sky.
Dilute the core
of some undiscovered world.

Each nail connects a thought.
Rafters fasten the foundation
to unsteady walls.
The house transforms
into an idea.

There is the gasoline
oozing from the wooden arteries.
We thought it fuel,
but it fooled us!

It left the oceans as ash
and filled the hollow sky ...
finally.

Crying Phenomes

Words stumble
like drunks
from the mouth.

Reluctant syllables
build shoddy houses.
They serve as a temporary respite,
but the rain leaks
and you cannot stay long.

These houses populate
a weary universe.
We speak to build shelters
which collapse.

But thoughts made verbal
and into something material ...
cannot die!

The Raven of Modern Life

Knocking
never stops.
Fingers curled and rapping
on sickly oak doors
bang incessantly.

Make it stop.
Finally.
Muted by car door slam.

Loud radio and coffee spill forget,
but under homework assignments
the knock is there.

Somewhere,
deep in the universe of the skull.
A knocking echo
among the brain planet
and starry veins.

My astronaut skin suspends.

There is no sound in space,
in the silent universe,
except knocking on
forgotten oak doors.

The old man
will never die.
He's lived
so much longer than me.
He keeps knocking.
He begs to be let in.

But I am too frightened
to open the door
locked and fused
beneath the tectonic plate
of the skull.

If You Look

I wonder what hides
in the airwaves.
What beast sleeps
in the numbers?

Climbing and counting, as it goes higher,
I speak a synecdoche of truth
with jigsaw sentence fragments
that sound important.

Hair, rocks and a yellow tooth
become poetry.

A type of metonymy
for the stupid to grasp
Like a tall oak tree.

Fools Love the Obvious

Fools love the obvious ...
but you have to sell it to them.

Idiots crave the words
they already know.
Crave them like bleach or fire or snow
at the end of the world.

But it's not the end.
No!

It's just a billboard.
A blog post.
A commercial.

This is all they know,
because they think
with borrowed thoughts
that are not their own.

Deposit

Like a dying star
I drive
on the highway, useless.
Away from my well lit town
I was,
the last hand crafted model
by God.

Now they are all standardized.
God can rest.
It's always the 7th day.
Standardized with some gaseous core.
The heart and fears.

I am obsolete.
An antique like the sun.

They can just make a new one.
It's so much cheaper,
Easier.

The factories pump
day and night,
under an artificial sun,
under a neon moon they made.

I could replace my bones
one by one
with your standardized parts:,
easier to maintain,
easier to discard.

Drive Back

I do not dream
of glorious ends.
I just suffer the means
to meet them.

Like a sentence
I refuse to inhabit.
A fabricated world.

Ghosts don't hold fast to nails.
Cannot fasten them down.

Ghost hammers have no echo,
just hands outstretched
with no wrist bone, waiting, waiting
for the communion tablet of the moon
solitary in its chalice sky.

Hungry ghosts devour the moon
like invisible cannibals
floating on rooftops,
salivating over
their unholy meal.

I can't trust them.

Route 81

We have all wanted the same things:
From log cabins,
And dumpsters.
 We have had the same dreams
in our comas.

I have always pondered
The movement of history:
In my own arm.
The bend in my knee.
Chicken bones in the trash.
Holes in my shoe.
This couch and all the eternities.
From my seat to the television.
All the sorrow in my spoon.
All the black space.
In my sweatshirt .
Under the hood.
Outside in the rain.

A thousand existences contained:
In the wet pavement.
In the snow.

In my cold breath
rising above
the rusty cars.

Here

I do not want to go upstairs
into that bedroom.
It has turned into hell
with shifting bedsheets
and broken windows.
Demons in the desk drawers.
Eyes in the ceiling. Veins in floor.
This lighted noisy basement
is safe for now.

But those awful stairs
could lead to a black hole
in the stomach of a dead star,
of a constellation stiff in postmortem glory.

It crawls on my white carpet
dragging its starry legs.
I am digested into a thought
an image, a second
that ticks away on your watch.

Forget it (you already have).
Forget the fear,
swallowed by those heavenly bodies
in short dresses sitting at their dinner tables.

They cannot see into my basement.
Into this temporary sanctuary.
But their telescopes are pointed at my bed
waiting for me to sleep.
They will throw those dead constellations
on top of me like bowling balls.
They want me to scream!

Christmas Tree Park

You don't know his name.
He doesn't win any awards.
He washes the floor
and he looks exactly the same
as the millions that came before.

He is not famous or trending
but he meticulously disassembles
the universe,
one quark at a time,
while pretending to care
about your awards.

The Unraveling

The bald tire
Unravels.

Metal fibers scrape
on an indifferent road.

The tire's body
is thrown in the shoulder lane,
forgotten.

When the tires' body realizes
there is no heaven,
it becomes a ghost
and wanders through hearts
and power lines
and all the things
you do not notice.

The Crucifixion

I want to become
electricity.
Dance incoherently
in brain stems
televisions
and power lines.

But there is electricity
inside me.
Maybe it's my soul
or residue from
the universes creation.

I want to commune with it;
with this unholy current, with this God.
I envy its lack of solidity;.
its ability to slip between
certain surfaces.

But even this awesome power
has a higher god.
A rubber god which denies it.
Perhaps we need to build rubber stars
and rubber brains
to contain this awful thing.
Bottle it up in a rubber ventricle.
Let it ricochet in a dying heart
pushed by old blood.

It is no longer intimidating
Let it die. Crucify it ...
and make way for a new god.

The People Before Us

I pulled the fridge from the wall
to clean the dirt from the compressor.
(I did not unplug it)
And I wondered,
did the people who owned the house before us
clean the compressor?

This fridge held 20 years of meals for them.
Pot roasts and chicken cutlets.
Do they even eat these things?
Maybe my family is just a copy of theirs.
Maybe we are just copies of each other
with newer phones
and different brains.

We need to continually clean the dirt
from the compressor fans
to ensure the universe still works.

Like a modern day Aztec
offering modern blood
to an updated sun.

Cynical

What is famous
is not what will be remembered
but is born
from dark
and atoms and big bangs,
reigns of dead kings
in ancient graves.

The sun remembers
and sears all of it.

Musing

Internalized lens of disposability
like glass shards in a soft brain
refracting accumulated misery
which is logged in food stamps
and free milk maybe you trade
for something more valuable
like a red sky on Mars.

But that will die too.

No one wants a red sky,
so drink your free milk
and shit out a new universe.

What We Will Become

He collects Cicada shells
and corn husks,
orange rinds and
peach pits.

He walks along the side
of some road
with a hole in his shoe
where the water seeps in.

He collects these things
because they remind him.

The Return

I met at the corners
joined with angles
perpendicular in their ability
to fasten a thought.

A geography of veins
wrapped in tin foil
ossify into dust
and cavities in the foundations;
cavities filled with
baptismal font bleach.

Just think!

There are millions
of bleached filled holes
underneath
your cities
and sturdy buildings.

The Unintended Consequences of Liberation

It's done.
She brushes her teeth.
Falls asleep on the bed.

The teeth
are like permanent medallions
of participation
in some erotic script
that replays ad nauseum
across multiple universes.

In one of those universes.
she messages a clone in North Dakota
to see the script again.
One more time.

And white film descends
like a repugnant sunset
all over again.

And I am left to wonder:
Why does liberation hurt so much?

Another Musing

Window candles flicker
in cigarette smoke
and hip hop music;
outfield dirt.

I need more pieces to make sense.
This is still incomplete .

Cloth jerseys,.
Cadillacs on pavement,
Concession stands,
span the universe.

What can I buy?
Soda? Peanuts?
A redoubt to defeat the onslaught
of pundits and stale truth?

Inaudible Trees

Are there secrets in the wind?
Swirling leaves dance
in a cosmic ballet
and whisper some truth
which no one cares for.

A dream in every house
offered on secret altars of clean bed sheets.

What if the sky is a mirror?

And grass an accountant which counts
all the crimes committed
even in our heads?

The SUV drinks earth's oil
while I brew her coffee.

Thanksgiving

Give thanks:

    For corners and receipts .

    Atoms of paper and plaster.

    Molecules that you forgot
    that splinter, reconstruct
    into bricks and winter.

    And an advertisement
    for a carpet.

Turn off the television.
Hit the button twice.
Give thanks
for a new universe.

But, I have been here before
in this room,
and, I choose to leave ...
again.

Peaking in November

Like a maple in autumn,
beautiful before death,
I look for a similarity in myself.

But all I find is empty water bottles
and slaughterhouses.
Toothaches and Christmas lights
which must be put away in January.

Before time
there was singularity
but now there is only me
walking home
on a cold day,
peaking in November.

The Time for Poets

There is a lamp
shining in the future.

I can see it now
but a tired, stubborn sun
refuses to die.

Inconsistent light
gives hope and laughs
as it strangles.
all we can become.

Some poets see the lamp
and laugh at the first sun
but the time for poets is done

   ... or is it?

Tennessee

Tennessee, stuck in my throat,
chocked like a peach pit,
unable to grow
over state lines

But capable
to reroute the blood
through time zone bones
so I can miss you
an hour earlier.

Where Are All the Windows?

Can you see the empty space?
Hear its echo in vacant houses
with broken windows?

No, you cannot.
It eludes you
because you are a peach pit:
       Dried and used of its nectar.
       Dried and used of its life.
       Brewing with the sadness
       of a billion people
       you never knew

The earth divorces its core.
The sun separates from its solar system.

I have whispered to
these lonely people
and they have revealed their pain
at the dinner table.

I am the broken femur of the Olympian,

Life Should Not Be Here

There are teeth in everything .
In the sign that reads
'Welcome to Cicero'
Growing calcium .

I steal energy
from the leaves.
I suck their green.

But still,
teeth grow jagged
from a Connecticut license plate,
from the guardrail
and highway marker;
and I am so afraid
the inanimate
will somehow figure out
how to live
and kill me.

So, I pray to the new teeth
that only I can see.
The teeth that bloom
in the double yellow line.

I Wait

Higher than a skyscraper
or any man-made thing
is where I exist .

Waiting ...
for that old priest,
with white hair
who holds his bible,
able to divorce me
from the only smile I have.

I wait for him
in this plane of existence
where the tired birds
can no longer hold me up.

Their beaks
are not strong enough.

The priest is gone
and I am crying .
Dreaming of guns and oil
of continents un-stapling themselves
from the ocean's floor
walking off the earth
in protest
hating their feet.

Dirty with rubber and dust
 ... and blood

Down

Guard me
with your oil,
halo.

Protect me
from the endless black holes
of the passenger seat,
of the barber's chair.

Re-align the spine
with a vertical sunbeam.

Pin me to the earth.
Make a straight line .
Keep me on the righteous path.

March me
like a machine
into the world
categorized to die
one of its appointed deaths.

Before I was to die
I promised my guardian
I would obey the world's traffic signs.

Stop and yield
to a sadness hardened permanently
in the asphalt road
leading to a black hole
somewhere in the universe.
beyond the restaurants
and shoe stores.

Somewhere further
than the stain on my tie.

The guardian of glass and steel
is my space suit protecting me,
the astronaut
from some hideous universe.

Morning

On the side of the road
I saw a used tire
pretending to be a world.

I have walked in this world
and many others like it.

I have enjoyed their company
and not felt lonely
in these fake universes.

Hack

Concrete bowels
under the George Washington bridge
stink like fumes,
dung from tailpipes.

These beasts
produce no milk.
Prime cut engine block cows
no Hindu would pray to.

They march over the bridge
from New York
to New Jersey and back again.

Unholy cows
marked as fords and Toyotas.

Cows that speak perfect English
reeking of body odor
with money clips.

Housewives stashing machetes
up their dress.

Processions of cars,
herded over the bridge
... home for dinner.

Orion's Secret

Australopithecines stand near erect.
Closer to the as of yet unnamed Orion
so they could listen to the star's secrets echo
in fires and embers and lightning strikes.

Shamans and priests wove the secrets
into constellations of black bodies and yellow teeth.
They then mapped these constellations
across a universe they did not know.

The secret is a gene
carried in human blood.

But it atrophies or bursts
like an appendix ... unnoticed.

New Church

The light switch in the basement
turns off the sun.
It's now like a bowling ball:
A sickly black sphere
suspended in the sky.

And the day is like night
but the night is brighter with a moon.

I want to be saved.
I pray.
But all I had to do
was love your heart more than
the red brick in my own chest.

Save me
from this slow apocalypse
in my bedroom,
as the lamp breaks
and the carpet runs with blood.

Now all the churches are gone.
The people, the houses, the windows
begin to unglue themselves,
extinguish like flames
but I am revived and ask for one thing:
A blowtorch

I desperately try to weld the universe back together,
viewed from my bedroom,
that I cannot see anymore.

Cosmic Poem

There is a box of thumbprints in the moon
collected from the past.

Glass memories notch their place
among the stars.
Kings in this hour during a lunar eclipse
blocking last year like chewed meat
in the windpipe of some sky or throat.

I can't breathe the night sky
through its black tar above.

Finally a sunrise with no sleep
and the memories die
on the side of some road
like animals, like squirrels or possums
in shallow puddles.
You wade in those puddles,
but I, as far away as a star
and as deep as the black hole
that star will become ,
black tar in the nose,
I am covered in this.

There is some sort of universe in my mouth.
The star implodes in unused veins.
The hair is gone, blood and clothes vanished.

But even I used to exist once ...
where nothing lives now.

The Important Things

There is so much cancer in the universe
and worn out pistons,
broken wrists
cannot make corners meet anymore.

Bleach drains off the glass
and is refracted in the door.

How many gods have died?
How many carpets are turned up
to find more water and gasoline,
more Octobers and clean furnaces
that power distant galaxies
whose civilizations will never know?

Gondwanaland

The scalding plum is a riddle
which portends some truth.

This rustic knowledge is lateral
and a sanctuary.

This knowledge is nerves scattered
in skin and crooked wax.

Oceans and echoes,
on broken continents,
pulsate in dreams
we never had.

.

Author Profile:

Angelo Letizia writes mainly speculative themed poetry and is currently a professor of education at a small college in Baltimore Maryland. His true passion however is poetry. *The Starry Devil and Other Unwanted Poems* is his debut book of poetry and his second book of poetry *ThePilgrim of Infinity* will be released in 2022.

Angelo's poetry has also been published in a number of literary outlets including *Tales from the Moonlit Path, Bewildering Stories, The Atlantean, Sirens Call, Red Planet, AHF Magazine, Dissections, Fevers of the Mind, Lothlorien Poetry Journal, Bindweed Magazine* and *Bowery Gothic* to name a few.

Angelo's academic credentials include:
- PhD. in Educational Policy Planning and Leadership, *College of William and Mary*
- MA. in European History, *Old Dominion University*
- BA. in Secondary Social Studies, *State University of New York* at Cortland

Angelo joined Notre Dame of Maryland in 2018 and currently teaches courses in Social Studies Methods, The History of American Education, The History of Higher Education, Educational Law, Action Research, Curriculum, Leadership Seminar, and Human Development and Learning. He has also taught courses in Cultural Diversity and Strategic Planning in the past.

Angelo lives with his wife and three children in Northern Maryland.

Acknowledgements

Two poems in this manuscript have appeared in other publications.

The poem New Church first appeared in the magazine *New American Legends*.

The poem Cosmic Poem first appeared in the magazine *New American Legends*.